Safely to Shore
America's Lighthouses

Iris Van Rynbach

Charlesbridge

In memory of my father, Jan D. Van Rynbach
— I. V. R.

Published by Charlesbridge
85 Main Street
Watertown, MA 02472
(617) 926-0329
www.charlesbridge.com

Library of Congress Cataloging-in-Publication Data

Van Rynbach, Iris.
  Safely to shore : America's lighthouses / Iris Van Rynbach.
    p. cm.
Summary: Describes the purpose and history of lighthouses, how they
work, who keeps them, and relates stories about famous American
lighthouses.
  ISBN 1-57091-434-6 (reinforced for library use) — ISBN 1-57091-435-4 (softcover)
  1. Lighthouses—United States—Juvenile literature. [1. Lighthouses.]
I. Title.
  VK1023 .V35 2003
  387.1'55'0973—dc21   2002010488

Printed in China
(hc) 10 9 8 7 6 5 4 3 2 1
(sc) 10 9 8 7 6 5 4 3 2 1

Illustrations done in watercolor and ink on Arches paper
Text type set in Cochin, display set in Bodoni and Bodoni Book
Color separations, printing, and binding by P. Chan & Edward, Inc.
Production supervision by Brian G. Walker
Designed by Susan Mallory Sherman

Hundreds of lighthouses dot America's coastline from east to west, north to south. Each has stories to tell of shipwrecks, rescues, and the unflagging determination of its keepers. Each lighthouse stands as a beautiful reminder of America's past and as a witness to the bravery of the men, women, and children who called the lighthouse home.

Sandy Hook Light
Sandy Hook, New Jersey • Built 1764

In the 1760s New York merchants donated money to build a lighthouse at the gateway to the majestic Hudson River. They hoped a great lighthouse would coax more ships into New York Harbor. Sandy Hook Light is the oldest original light tower in the United States.

On August 7, 1789, the first U. S. Congress established the National Lighthouse Service to maintain and oversee the country's lighthouses. It became the Lighthouse Board in 1852 and the Bureau of Lighthouses in 1910. In 1939 the U. S. Coast Guard took over its responsibilities. The Coast Guard now uses advanced technology to update and maintain hundreds of beacons from coast to coast.

Cape Disappointment Light

Cape Disappointment, Washington • Built 1856

In 1853 the ship *Oriole* was bringing building materials for the Cape Disappointment Light from the East Coast when it ran aground only two miles from the lighthouse site. The crew was rescued, but all the supplies were lost. New supplies arrived several months later, but thick mud slowed down the oxen that carried the materials up the cape's steep cliff. The tower was finally completed in 1854, but it took another two years for the lighthouse lens to be delivered. When it arrived at Cape Disappointment, the workmen discovered that the lens was too big for the tower. The lighthouse had to be torn down and rebuilt. It is now the oldest lighthouse still in use in the Pacific Northwest.

Scotch Cap Lighthouse
Scotch Cap, Alaska • Built 1903

Scotch Cap was Alaska's first lighthouse. It was built on the Pacific Ocean to mark the Unimak Pass into the Bering Sea. The keepers' families were not permitted to live in such an isolated location, so the keepers only saw their wives and children when they were on leave, once every four years. On April 1, 1946, tragedy struck. A tsunami, or tidal wave, swept the station into the sea, and all five keepers on duty were lost. In 1950 the Coast Guard constructed a new tower 116 feet above the icy water.

What makes a lighthouse?

Lighthouses stand on islands,
harbor entrances, offshore reefs,
shallow sandbars, and high, rocky
bluffs. The earliest lighthouses were
made of wood, stone, granite, or brick.
Some consisted of a single light tower.
Others were large compounds that
included a cottage for the keeper,
stables, chicken coops, and many
outbuildings.

In the 1850s cast-iron lighthouses
were manufactured and floated by ship
to their foundations. Some modern
lighthouses are built on massive piles
of steel driven 150 feet into the seabed.
A helicopter pad, a light tower, and a
radio beacon have replaced winding
stairs and chicken coops.

Chicago Harbor Light
Chicago, Illinois • Built 1893

In 1831 the original Chicago Harbor Light collapsed only hours after it was completed. It was quickly rebuilt, and throughout the 19th century renovations and replacements kept the lighthouse shining. The tower that stands today was put up in 1893, the year of the Columbian Exposition, or world's fair. At that time Chicago was one of the busiest ports in the country. Freighters sailed along Lake Michigan to unload timber, grain, and corn.

Thomas Point Shoal Light
Annapolis, Maryland • Built 1875

The Thomas Point lighthouse stands on the shoals of Chesapeake Bay. In the mid-19th century, engineers built lighthouses with wood and metal. First they stuck a heavy anchor deep into the seafloor. Then they fastened wooden poles to the anchor and used the poles to form the structure's base. The lighthouse perched on the base on thin metal legs, like a big spider. Thomas Point Shoal Light is the only one of this kind still at its original site today.

St. Augustine Lighthouse

Anastasia Island, Florida • Built 1874

The 165-foot spiral-striped brick lighthouse on Anastasia Island houses a powerful first-order Fresnel lens that lights the waterways around the old city of St. Augustine. In 1876 a Victorian-style keepers' house was built on the site. Three different lighthouse workers' families made it their home. The head keeper and the first assistant keeper each had a wing of the house for their families, but the second assistant keeper lived in just two small rooms on the top floor. The keepers' house was remodeled several times by the families who lived and worked there; indoor plumbing was added in 1907 and electricity in 1925. Eleven years later the lighthouse itself also switched to electricity. In 1970 the keepers' house was badly damaged by fire. Today the handsome brick house and lighthouse tower have been restored and are open to the public as a museum.

What makes the light?

In ancient times open fires warned sailors away from a rocky coast. Later sailors relied on lamps fueled by wood, coal, kerosene, or candles.

In 1822 French physicist Augustin-Jean Fresnel designed a new kind of reflector that used a series of glass circles to bend and concentrate light in a single, bright beam. Fresnel invented seven sizes, or orders. The order indicated the distance of the flame from the lens. In the first-order lens, the flame is farthest away and the light is brightest. Fresnel lenses became standard in most American lighthouses by the start of the Civil War.

During the 1920s and 1930s, most lighthouses converted to electric power. Today the Coast Guard uses plastic lenses molded in the Fresnel style around six or more small lightbulbs.

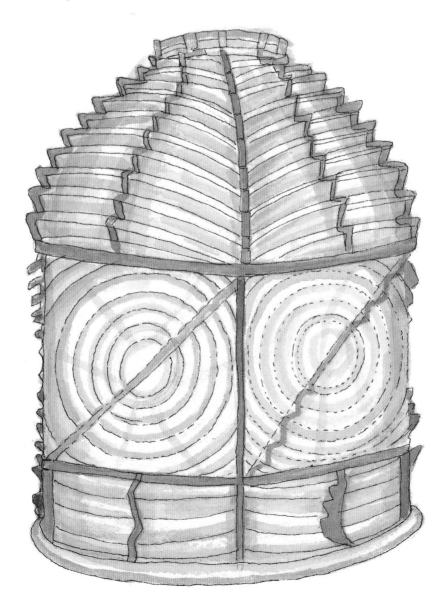

Umpqua River Lighthouse
Winchester Bay, Oregon • Built 1894

In 1983 the machinery that rotated the red-and-white flashing Fresnel lens of Umpqua River Lighthouse broke down. The Coast Guard wanted to replace the lens with a modern beacon, but local citizens persuaded the Coast Guard to restore the antique first-order lens instead. The classic lens, first lit in 1894, is still in use today.

Split Rock Lighthouse
Lake Superior, Minnesota • Built 1910

Split Rock Lighthouse perches 168 feet above the cold water of the western reaches of Lake Superior. The first keepers had to wear dark goggles and avoid the lantern deck when the giant third-order Fresnel lens was in motion. Its glare, visible 22 miles over the lake, could damage their eyesight. The huge lens weighed more than four tons and had 252 glass panels. At 10-second intervals, the beam flashed on and off in the busy shipping lanes of Lake Superior.

Matinicus Rock Lighthouse
Rockland, Maine • Built 1827

Abbie Burgess lived at the Matinicus Rock Lighthouse and helped her father, the lighthouse keeper, with his work. In the winter of 1856, 17-year-old Abbie was left in charge while her father was away buying supplies. A fierce storm pounded the tiny island, cutting off Abbie, her sick mother, and her three young sisters from the mainland for nearly four weeks.

As the storm raged, Abbie wisely moved her family from their small cottage into the light tower itself. She rescued the hens from the henhouse minutes before the building was swept into the sea, and fed her family with the eggs the hens laid. For days she carried the heavy oil buckets up and down the steep stairs, trimmed the wicks, and cleaned the smoke from the glass so that the light would shine as brightly as it could.

Abbie never let the lights fail during the terrible storm. Sea captains who made their way into port were able to tell Abbie's despairing father that the lights were still burning at Matinicus Rock.

Abbie eventually married a lighthouse keeper and took care of lighthouses for the rest of her life. Her gravestone is a miniature model of a lighthouse.

What if you can't see the light?

Even the brightest light could be smothered by thick fog or swirling snow. Lighthouse keepers used cannons, guns, sirens, steam whistles, trumpets, and bells to warn sailors with sound in addition to light.

The first fog signal cannon in the United States was installed on Little Brewster Island in Boston Harbor in 1719. The second keeper of the Boston Lighthouse, John Hayes, came up with the idea of a cannon blast when he heard ships firing guns in the air so that they wouldn't collide in the fog. The Boston Lighthouse signal cannon was fired every half hour in foggy weather.

Boston Lighthouse
Boston, Massachusetts • Built 1716

Boston Lighthouse was built on Little Brewster Island at the entrance of Boston Harbor. It was the first lighthouse in the United States. The British blew it up during the Revolutionary War, and a new tower, pictured here, was built in 1783. Today this lighthouse is the only one in the United States with live-in lighthouse keepers.

Angel Island Light Station
Angel Island, California • Built 1886

The Angel Island Light Station was first established as a fog-bell signal station. The 4,000-pound fog bell was the largest in service at the time and was sounded by an automatic striking machine. Most machines would strike for 10,000 blows with one winding. But at fogged-in Angel Island, the fog bell averaged two blows every 15 seconds—11,520 rings per day! The striking machine had to be wound twice each day if the fog did not clear.

In 1906 Juliet Nichols was keeper of Angel Island Light Station. One day thick fog rolled into San Francisco Bay, and Juliet rushed to turn on the fog signal. But the striking machine broke down after only a few minutes. Juliet stared out into the fog. She could just make out the sound of slapping waves on a ship's hull. There was no time to fix the equipment, so Juliet grabbed a hammer and started pounding the fog bell. The ship heard the signal and veered away from the dangerous coast. Juliet was exhausted, but she knew she couldn't stop until the fog lifted. For 20 hours and 35 minutes, she struck the bell over and over until her arm ached and her ears rang. Juliet kept the Angel Island Light Station for 12 years. Her courage and dedication saved countless lives.

Who were the keepers?

People from every walk of life became lighthouse keepers. A keeper's job was secure as long as the work was done well. The pay was meager, but it sustained a simple lifestyle.

A keeper's life could be lonely and tedious, interrupted by periods of dangerous excitement if a ship foundered nearby or a storm pounded the coastline. Every day, the keeper wrote in a logbook to keep track of supplies, changing weather conditions, and daily events.

New London Ledge Lighthouse
New London, Connecticut • Built 1909

A keeper named Ernie Randolph was so dedicated to New London Ledge Lighthouse that his ghost is said to haunt the tower. When the Coast Guard took over the lighthouse in the 1940s, strange things began to happen. Lights mysteriously lit up. The foghorn was turned on and off at unusual times. Tools disappeared—and a scraping sound and soft footsteps were heard at the top of the lighthouse stairs.

Kilauea Point Light

Kilauea, Hawaii • Built 1913

In the 1920s Native Hawaiian keeper
Fred Robbins astonished visitors at Kilauea
Point Light by plunging into the shark-
infested waters of Kilauea National Wildlife
Refuge. He swam to an offshore islet called
Mokuaeae Rock and scaled a large boulder
there. Because he followed his ancestors'
beliefs and revered a shark god, Robbins
was fearless in the dangerous waters.

Pea Island Lifesaving Station

Pea Island, North Carolina • Built 1878

On October 11, 1896, the all-black
lifesaving crew at Pea Island performed a
daring rescue of the schooner *E. S. Newman*.
Led by the first African-American keeper,
Richard Etheridge, the surfmen braved
dangerous waters to bring all nine of the
schooner's crewmen to safety. In 1996 the
U.S. Coast Guard awarded the Gold Life
Saving Medal to Richard Etheridge and his
crew—a recognition that was long overdue.

Husbands, wives, and children all worked together at the lighthouse. They freshened the paint on the lighthouse, raked the sandy soil into neat rows, and planted carrots, peas, and tomatoes. All kinds of animals lived on the lighthouse grounds, too. Often the widow or family members of the keeper would be given the keeper's job in the event of his death. The keeper and his family were treated with great respect. Their hard work and dedication was recognized by all who depended on them along the coastal waters.

Biloxi Light
Biloxi, Mississippi • Built 1848

For years a mother-and-daughter team took care of Mississippi's Biloxi Light on the Gulf of Mexico. Maria Younghans was the keeper from 1867 to 1919, and her daughter Miranda tended the lighthouse from 1919 to 1929.

Elba Island Range Light Station
Elba Island, Georgia • Built 1884

During the late 1800s a disabled Civil War veteran named George Martus and his sister Florence kept the two Elba Island lights at the mouth of the Savannah River. In 1887 Florence fell in love with a Navy lieutenant from Cape Cod. When he left, she was heartbroken. Florence began to wave a white neckerchief he had given her at every ship that passed by the lighthouse, hoping her love might see it. A statue of Florence at the entrance of Savannah Harbor still greets passing ships.

Bolivar Point Light
Galveston, Texas • Built 1872

On September 8, 1900, a powerful hurricane devastated the area around the Bolivar Peninsula. The winding lighthouse steps were filled with more than 100 people taking refuge from the storm. Floodwater rushed into the lower part of the brick-lined iron lighthouse tower. During the hurricane keeper Harry Claiborne kept watch over the light, clinging to the handholds of the reeling tower. After the storm Claiborne and his wife fed everyone boiled beans and bread.

Lime Rock Lighthouse

Newport, Rhode Island • Built 1854

On March 29, 1869, three soldiers from Fort Adams were thrown into the sea when their boat capsized in Narragansett Bay. The keeper of Lime Rock had been ill for many years, and his daughter, Ida Lewis, had unofficially taken over his duties. Ida was an excellent rower and swimmer. She heard the men's cries and ran for her lifeboat. Ida rowed bravely out into the gale to pull the exhausted soldiers from the freezing water.

That year the Fourth of July was "Ida Lewis Day" in Newport. Crowds of flag-waving girls in starched linen dresses, sailors with their caps in hand, and grateful sea captains' wives honored Ida with a grand parade. They gave Ida a sleek mahogany rowboat with platinum-plated oarlocks and crimson velvet cushions. Even President Ulysses Grant showed up to congratulate her.

Ida performed many daring rescues throughout her career and became one of the most famous lighthouse keepers in America. In 1924, 13 years after Ida's death, the Rhode Island Legislature renamed Lime Rock "Ida Lewis Rock." Three years later the buildings on the site were sold and became the Ida Lewis Yacht Club. The light is still used as a private aid to navigation.

How are lighthouses used today?

There are more than 500 working lighthouses in the United States today, but most modern keepers now go ashore at the end of the day. They have electricity, radios, and radar to help them with their jobs. Sophisticated machines have replaced many keepers altogether. Humidity sensors operate foghorns, solar panels power the lights, light sensors turn beacons on and off, and automatic bulb changers replace burned-out bulbs.

Other lighthouses stand empty, but they continue to hold a special place in our history and in our hearts. With the help of local historical societies, many lighthouses have been restored to their original condition. Some have become museums, visitor centers, and even hotels.

Montauk Point Lighthouse
Montauk, New York • Built 1796

In 1998 the Montauk Point Lighthouse Museum Committee, part of the Montauk Historical Society, sponsored a major restoration of Montauk Point Lighthouse, at the eastern tip of Long Island. Contractors replaced the metal supports that hold up the lighthouse, added new mortar to the exterior walls, removed the old paint with a strong blast of baking soda, and applied special new paint to withstand the elements. Today the lighthouse houses a popular maritime museum, featuring an interactive diorama and the clam-shaped lens used in the tower from 1904 to 1987.

Cape Hatteras Lighthouse
Outer Banks, North Carolina • Built 1870

Cape Hatteras Lighthouse is 210 feet tall—the tallest lighthouse in the United States. It looks like a giant barber's pole. In 1999 the Coast Guard turned over the management of the lighthouse to the National Park Service, and the lighthouse became a National Historic Landmark. But the sand around the tower had eroded, and the lighthouse was in danger of falling into the sea. To preserve it, the tower was moved 2,900 feet farther inland, southwest from its original location. The lighthouse now stands the same distance from the water as when it was first built—about 1,600 feet from the water's edge.

Cape Neddick Light

York Beach, Maine • Built 1879

Russ Ahlgren was the last keeper of Cape Neddick Light, popularly called Nubble Lighthouse, before the station was automated in July 1987. Living as a keeper made everyday household chores a challenge. Just getting back and forth to the mainland in the three-person rubber life raft was difficult, because the boat could tip over in more than two feet of surf.

The boat was so small that the Ahlgren family had to devise another way of getting groceries out to the lighthouse. Russ's wife, Brenda, would buy a month's worth of groceries at a time, bring them to the water's edge, and place them in a wooden box suspended from a cable. By hand, Russ and Brenda would pull the box across the water to the island, where Russ would unload the food into a cart. Then Russ and their son, Chris, would row the raft over to the mainland to bring Brenda back.

Like many keepers before them, the Ahlgrens had several daily chores. Every three hours between 6:00 A.M. and 6:00 P.M., Russ took readings of visibility, wind speed and direction, wave height, barometric pressure, and temperature. Then he sent the detailed weather report to Portsmouth Harbor Station. Russ and Brenda also made sure the lighthouse light was turned on and working properly.

Portland Head Light
Portland, Maine • Built 1790

On January 10, 1791, lighthouse keeper Joseph Greenleaf climbed the stairs to light the whale oil lamp of Portland Head Light for the first time. He began a tradition that lasted almost 200 years. From whale oil to kerosene to electric bulbs and automated switches, Portland Head Light and its keepers adjusted to the changing technology of the times.

On August 7, 1989, a crowd of 600 people watched as Coast Guard Petty Officer Davis Simpson, the last keeper of Portland Head Light, lowered the flag for the very last time. The decommissioning ceremony ended when Portland Head's horn sounded three loud blasts over the water, and the lightship *Nantucket* echoed its salute to the men, women, and children who kept the light burning for 198 years. Portland Head Light now serves a new role, as a museum dedicated to the history of local lighthouses.

Each year thousands of people visit the nation's lighthouses to learn about the vital role they played in our history. The innumerable lives saved and ships rescued throughout their long history are a testament to these coastal guardians and keepers of the light.

Books for younger readers

Women of the Lights by Candace Fleming (Morton Grove, IL: Albert Whitman, 1996).

Beacons of Light by Gail Gibbons (New York: Morrow Junior Books, 1990).

Lighthouse: Living in a Great Lakes Lighthouse 1910-1940 by Megan O'Hara (Mankato, MN: Blue Earth Books, 1998).

Sink or Swim: African-American Lifesavers of the Outer Banks by Carol Boston Weatherford (Wilmington, NC: Coastal Carolina Press, 1999).

Books for older readers

Women Who Kept the Lights: An Illustrated History of Female Lighthouse Keepers by Mary Louise Clifford and J. Candace Clifford (Williamsburg, VA: Cypress Communications, 1993).

Guardians of the Lights: The Men and Women of the U.S. Lighthouse Service by Elinor DeWire (Sarasota, FL: Pineapple Press, 1995).

Legendary Lighthouses: The Companion to the PBS Television Series by John Grant and Ray Jones (Old Saybrook, CT: Globe Pequot Press, 1998).

Endangered Lighthouses: Stories and Images of America's Disappearing Lighthouses by Tim Harrison and Ray Jones (Guilford, CT: Globe Pequot Press, 2001).

Web sites

(Remember that Web sites can change, so try running a search on "lighthouses" using your favorite search engine.)

The Maritime Heritage Program, Lighthouse Heritage

http://www.cr.nps.gov/maritime/lt_index.htm
Maintained by the National Park Service. Offers information on lighthouse history, publicly-accessible lighthouses by region, and lighthouse preservation.

The U.S. Coast Guard: Lighthouses, Lightships, and Aids to Navigation

http://www.uscg.mil/hq/g-cp/history/h_lhindex.html
Includes a chronology of the U.S. Lighthouse Service and a photo gallery of lighthouses.

The Lighthouse Directory

http://www.unc.edu/~rowlett/lighthouse
Maintained by the University of North Carolina. Provides a directory of lighthouses around the world, as well as other lighthouse links.

Lighthouses in this book